GRAPHIC LIBRARY™

STEM ADVENTURES

THE REMARKABLE WORLD OF ROBOTS

MAX AXIOM
STEM ADVENTURES

by Agnieszka Biskup

illustrated by Pixelpop Studios

D1456232

CAPSTONE PRESS
a capstone imprint

Graphic Library is published by Capstone Press,
1710 Roe Crest Drive, North Mankato, Minnesota 56003
www.capstonepub.com

Library of Congress Cataloging-in-Publication Data
Names: Biskup, Agnieszka, author.
Title: The remarkable world of robots / by Agnieszka Biskup.
Description: North Mankato, Minnesota : Capstone Press, 2018. | Series:
    Graphic library. STEM adventures | Series: Max Axiom STEM adventures |
    Audience: Age 8–14. | Audience: Grade 4 to 6. | Includes bibliographical
    references and index.
Identifiers: LCCN 2017008337| ISBN 9781515773917 (library binding)
    ISBN 9781515773979 (paperback) | ISBN 9781515773993 (ebook PDF)
Subjects: LCSH: Robots—Juvenile literature. | Robots—Comic books, strips,
    etc. | Graphic novels.
Classification: LCC TJ211.2 .B57 2018 | DDC 629.8/92—dc23
LC record available at https://lccn.loc.gov/2017008337

Designer
Steve Mead

Cover Artist
Pixelpop Studios

Colorist
TOMMY ADI HUTOMO

Media Researcher
Wanda Winch

Production Specialist
Steve Walker

Editor
Mari Bolte

Printed in the United States of America.
3114

TABLE OF CONTENTS

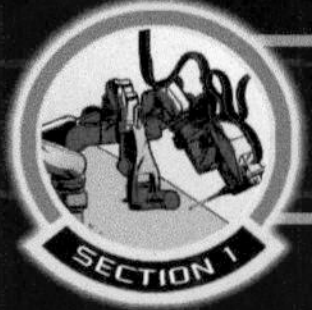
SECTION 1

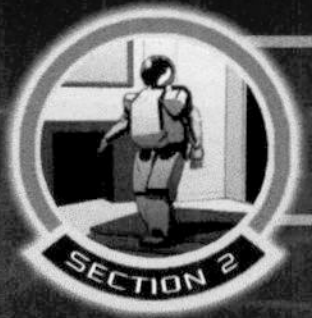
SECTION 2

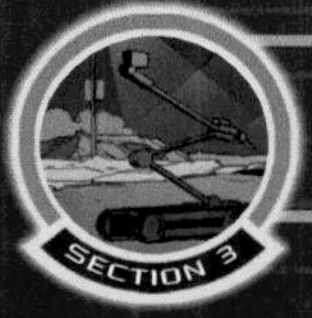
SECTION 3

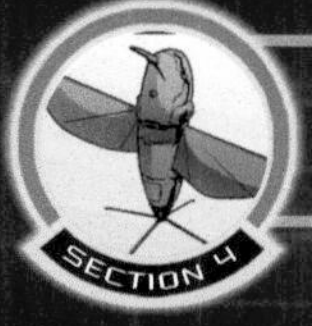
SECTION 4

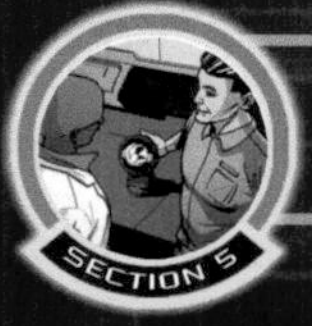
SECTION 5

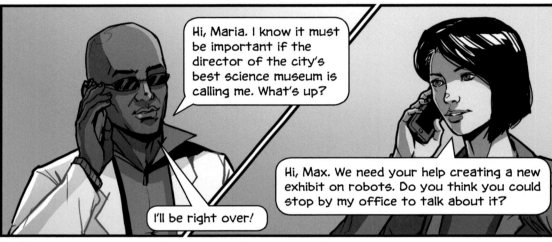

THE FIRST ROBOT

The word robot comes from the Czech word for work: *robota*. It was first used in a 1920 science fiction play by Czech writer Karel Capek called *R.U.R. (Rossum's Universal Robots)*. The first robot shown on film was in Fritz Lang's *Metropolis* (1927).

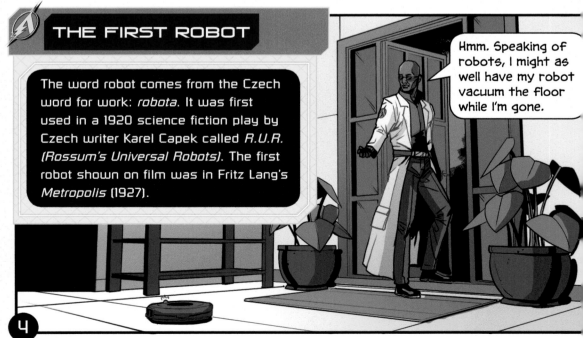

So how can I help?

We want people to know more about what robots really are.

When most people think of a robot, they imagine the ones we see in sci-fi movies, TV shows, and video games. But there are robots all around us.

So, you're creating an exhibit about the nuts and bolts behind robots.

That's right. We'd like you to gather as much information as you can.

The sooner you can get started the better.

I'm on the case!

Thanks for your help, Max.

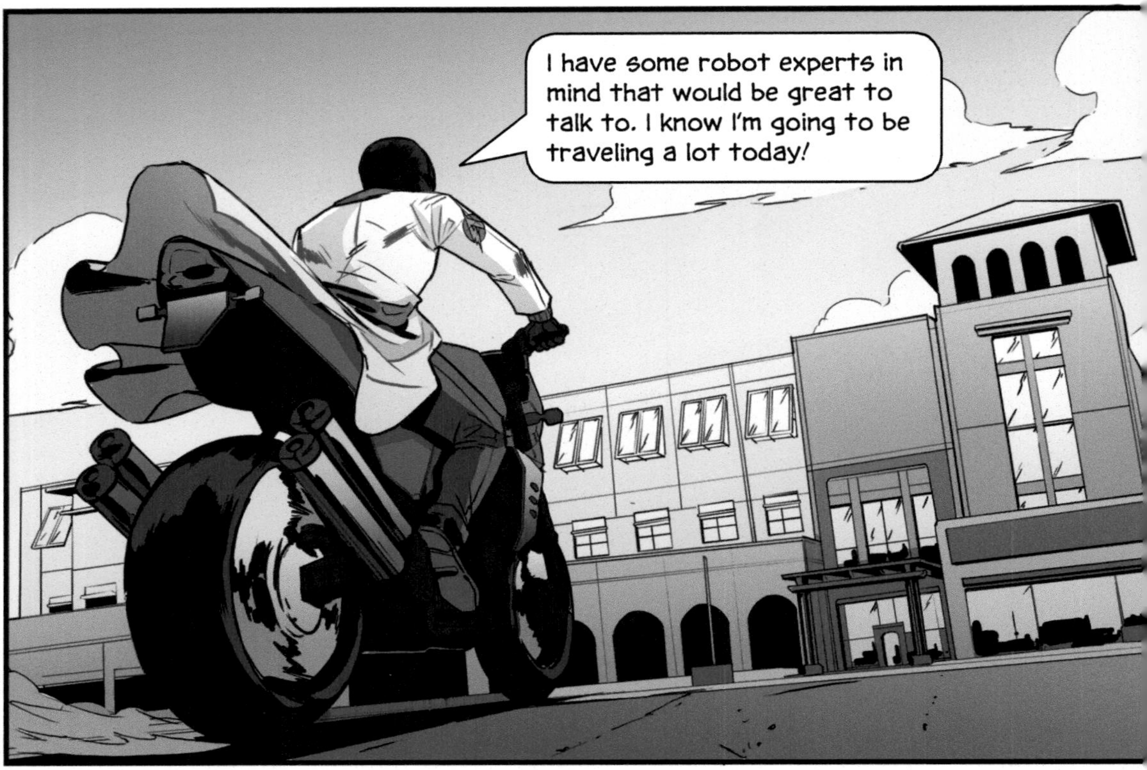
I have some robot experts in mind that would be great to talk to. I know I'm going to be traveling a lot today!

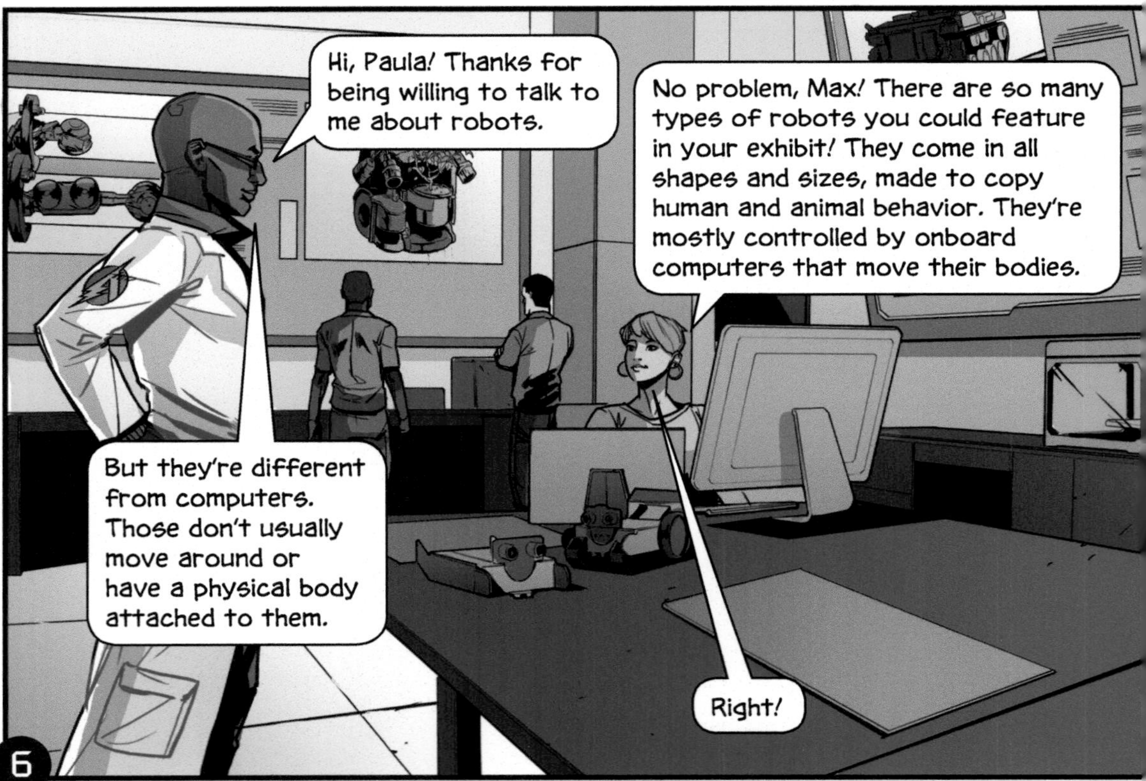
Hi, Paula! Thanks for being willing to talk to me about robots.
No problem, Max! There are so many types of robots you could feature in your exhibit! They come in all shapes and sizes, made to copy human and animal behavior. They're mostly controlled by onboard computers that move their bodies.
But they're different from computers. Those don't usually move around or have a physical body attached to them.
Right!

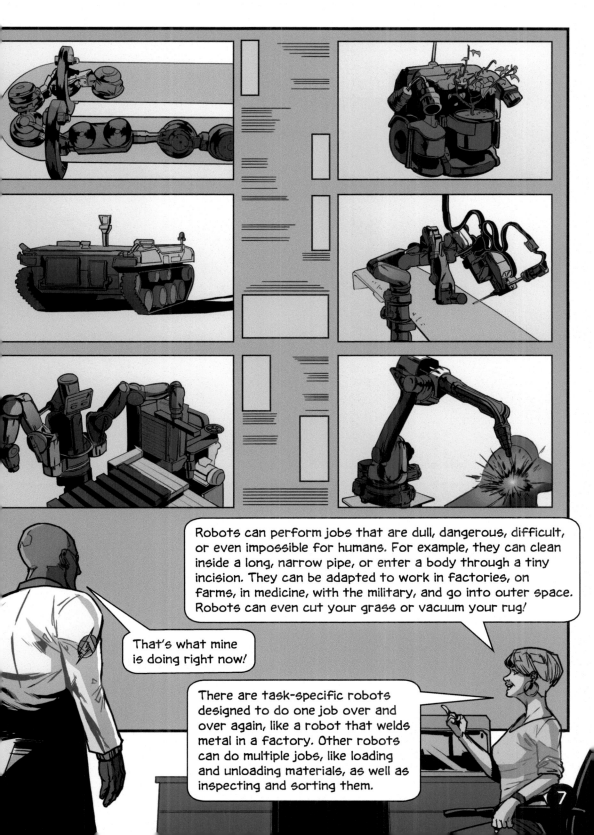

Robots can perform jobs that are dull, dangerous, difficult, or even impossible for humans. For example, they can clean inside a long, narrow pipe, or enter a body through a tiny incision. They can be adapted to work in factories, on farms, in medicine, with the military, and go into outer space. Robots can even cut your grass or vacuum your rug!

That's what mine is doing right now!

There are task-specific robots designed to do one job over and over again, like a robot that welds metal in a factory. Other robots can do multiple jobs, like loading and unloading materials, as well as inspecting and sorting them.

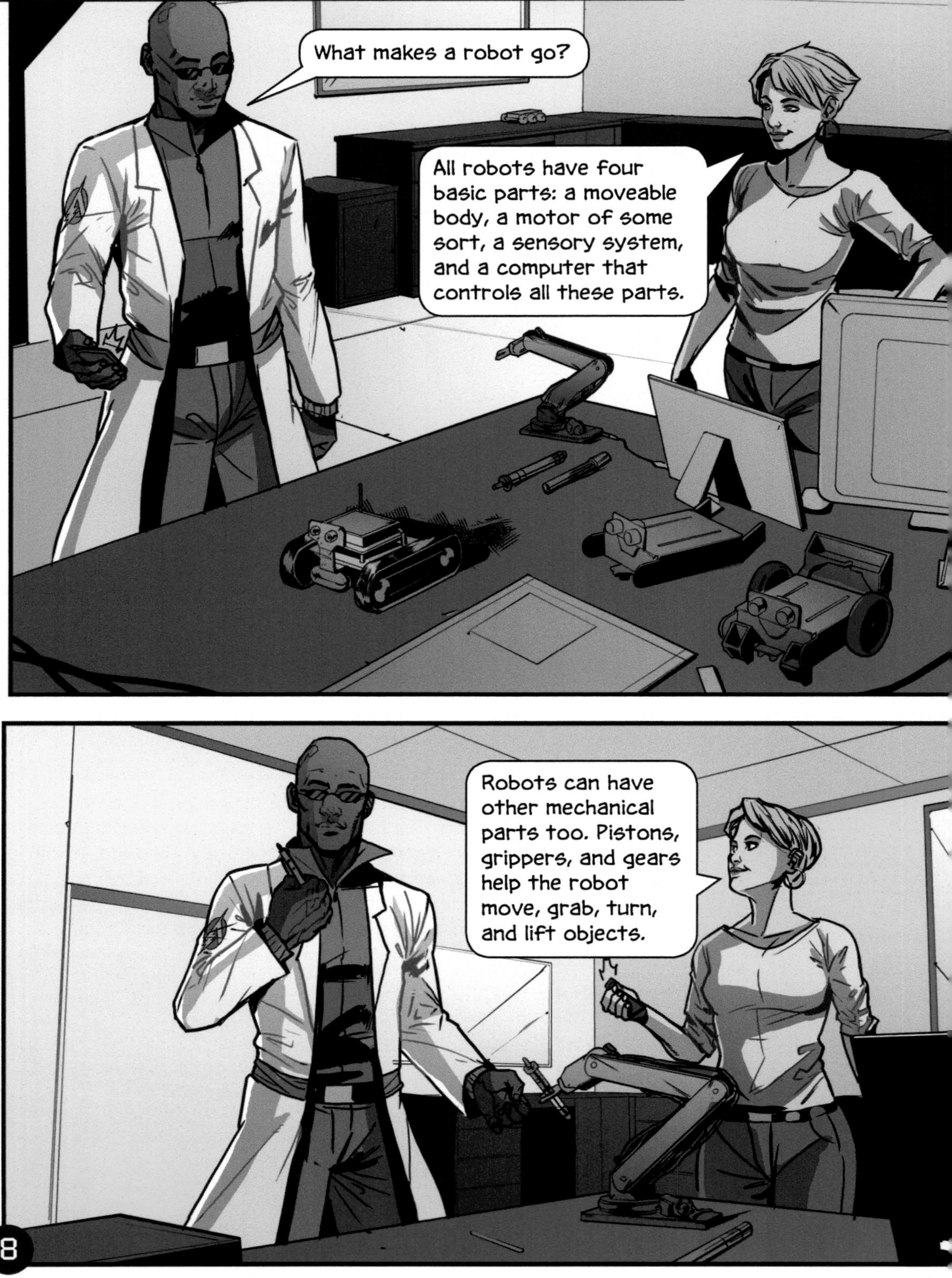
What makes a robot go?
All robots have four basic parts: a moveable body, a motor of some sort, a sensory system, and a computer that controls all these parts.
Robots can have other mechanical parts too. Pistons, grippers, and gears help the robot move, grab, turn, and lift objects.

Some robots have motorized wheels that help them move around.

Wow! That one has movable segments connected by joints. They're just like the joints that connect the bones in our bodies.

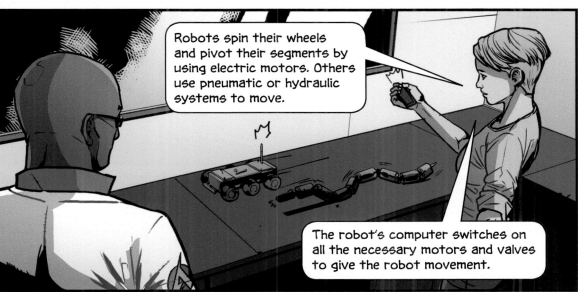

Robots spin their wheels and pivot their segments by using electric motors. Others use pneumatic or hydraulic systems to move.

The robot's computer switches on all the necessary motors and valves to give the robot movement.

HYDRAULIC AND PNEUMATIC SYSTEMS

Some robots use hydraulic or pneumatic systems to move. In pneumatic systems, pressurized air is used to produce movement. In hydraulic systems, trapped, pressurized water forces movement instead.

Robots also need some kind of power source to drive these systems. This small robot uses a battery.

My vacuum robot at home plugs itself into the wall to charge its battery.

A robot has sensors that allow it to examine its surroundings.

Like humans, robots are able to take in feedback and react. Is an area hot or cold? Is there an object in the way? What is the best way around that object? Those are the kinds of things our senses tell us.

The most common robotic sense is the robot's ability to monitor how it moves. This robot can identify the right amount of pressure so it won't crush my hand.

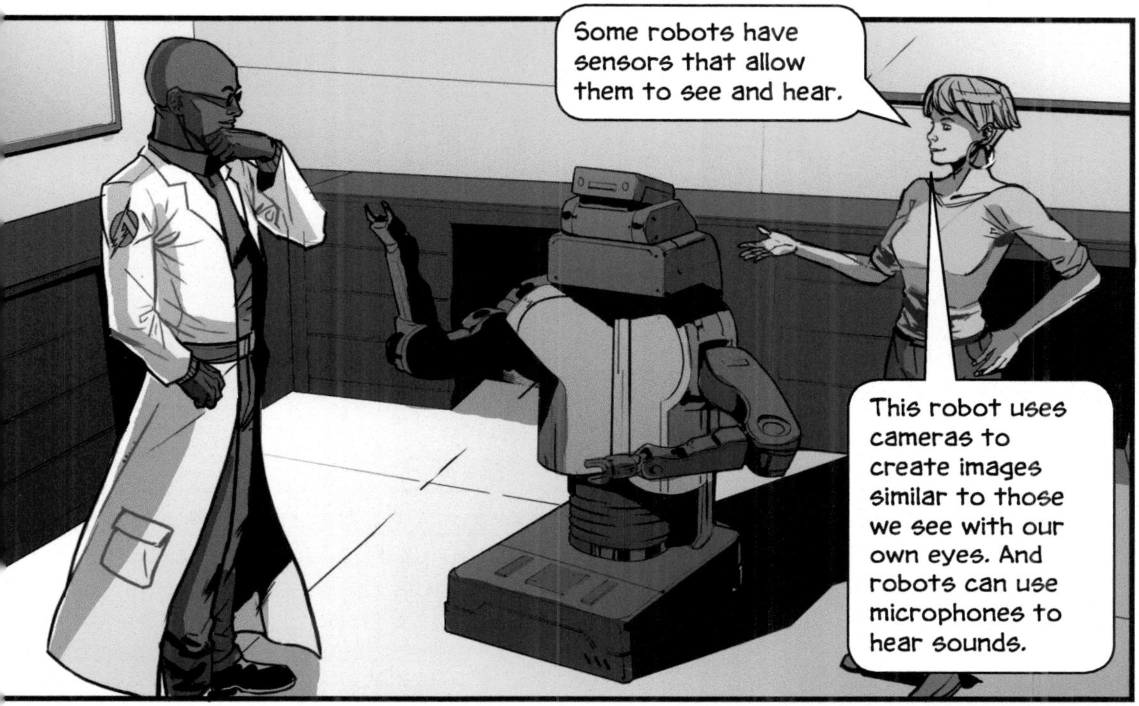
Some robots have sensors that allow them to see and hear.
This robot uses cameras to create images similar to those we see with our own eyes. And robots can use microphones to hear sounds.

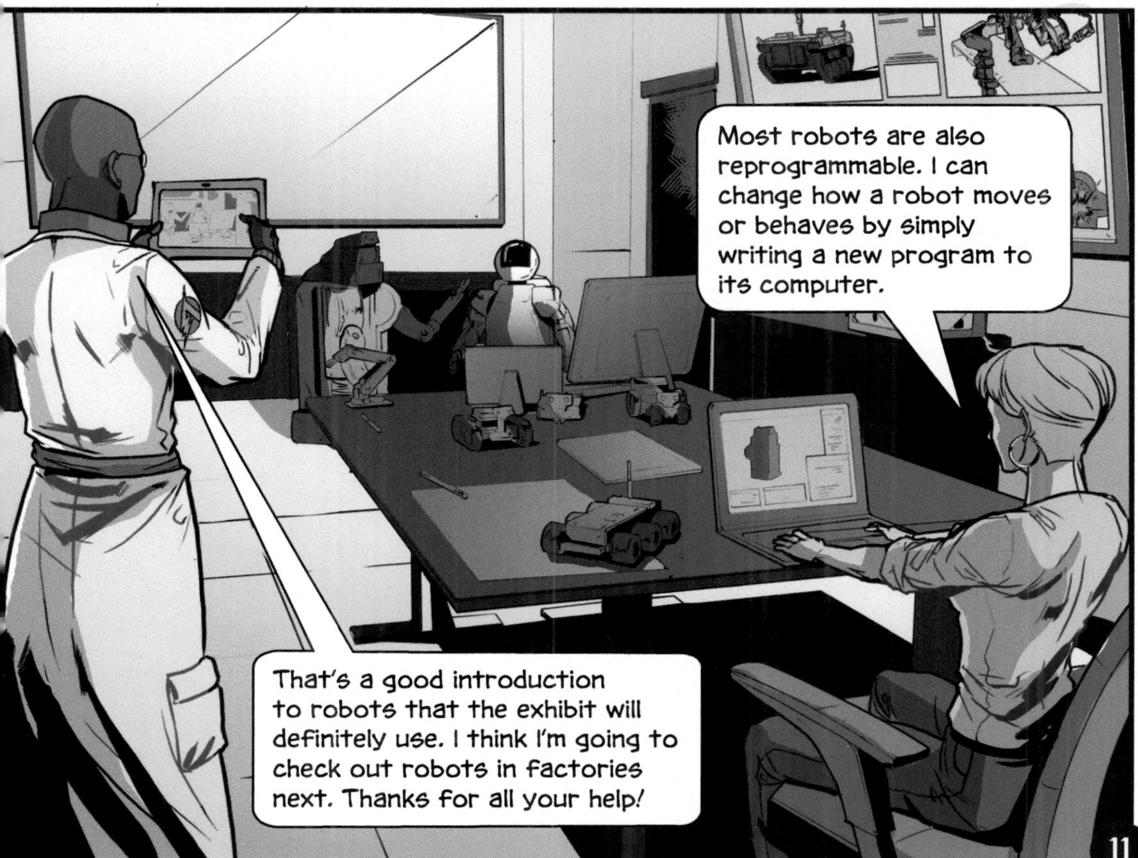
Most robots are also reprogrammable. I can change how a robot moves or behaves by simply writing a new program to its computer.
That's a good introduction to robots that the exhibit will definitely use. I think I'm going to check out robots in factories next. Thanks for all your help!

INDUSTRIAL, MOBILE, AND MILITARY ROBOTS

Today robots are commonly used in factories. Let's see how robots work in the auto industry. This will be an important part of the exhibit.

Hi, Max. Welcome to our completely automated car assembly line! We have hundreds of robots putting cars together

A car is welded, glued, spray painted, and assembled on a conveyor. Robots work at each station. They can even inspect for defects.

The robots use lasers and cameras to fit windshields, door panels, and fenders together.

Robots in our plant also pack and unpack items, and load, unload, and transport goods. They really do all the heavy lifting.

The first industrial robot, Unimate, was a 4000-pound programmable robotic arm. General Motors used Unimate in 1961 in its auto assembly line. It took die castings from machines and welded auto bodies.

Thanks, Jack! Now that I've seen what robot arms can do on a factory floor, I want to check out completely mobile bots.

13

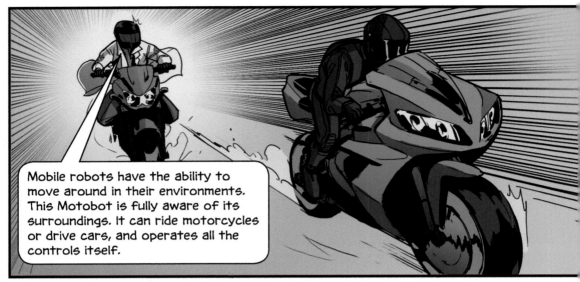

Mobile robots have the ability to move around in their environments. This Motobot is fully aware of its surroundings. It can ride motorcycles or drive cars, and operates all the controls itself.

This remote-controlled bot uses sensors and previously-programm controls to perform tasks for me

I can tell it to pick up a ball, but the robot can figure out where the ball is and the best method to grab it.

Remote-controlled robots can be used for exploring the deep sea . . .

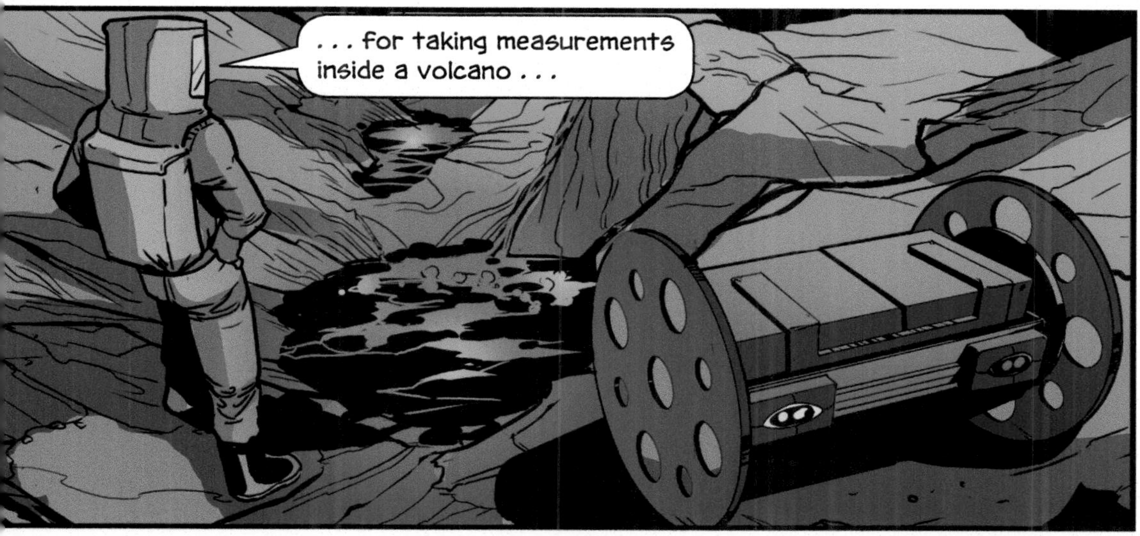
. . . for taking measurements inside a volcano . . .

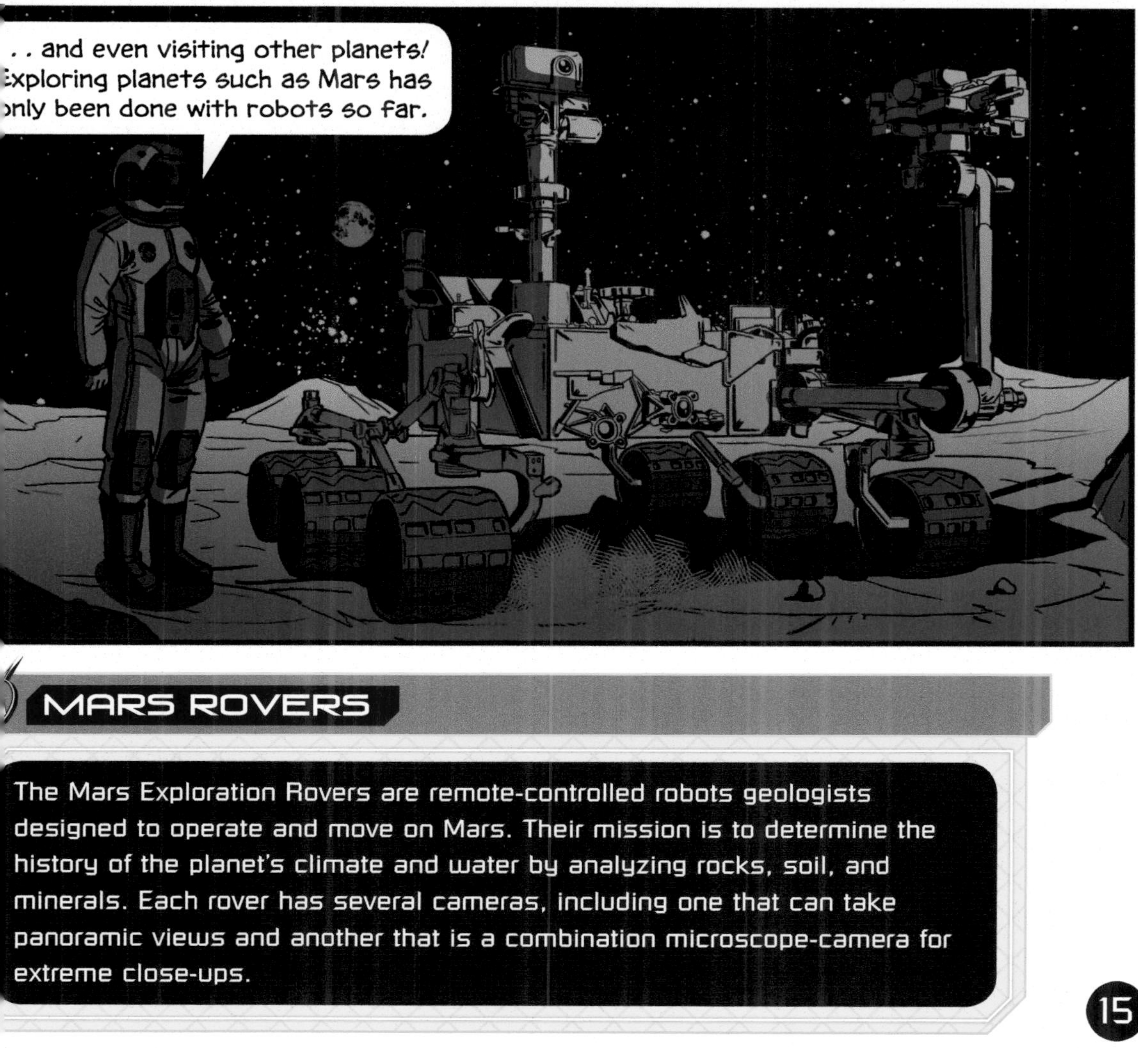
. . and even visiting other planets! xploring planets such as Mars has nly been done with robots so far.

MARS ROVERS

The Mars Exploration Rovers are remote-controlled robots geologists designed to operate and move on Mars. Their mission is to determine the history of the planet's climate and water by analyzing rocks, soil, and minerals. Each rover has several cameras, including one that can take panoramic views and another that is a combination microscope-camera for extreme close-ups.

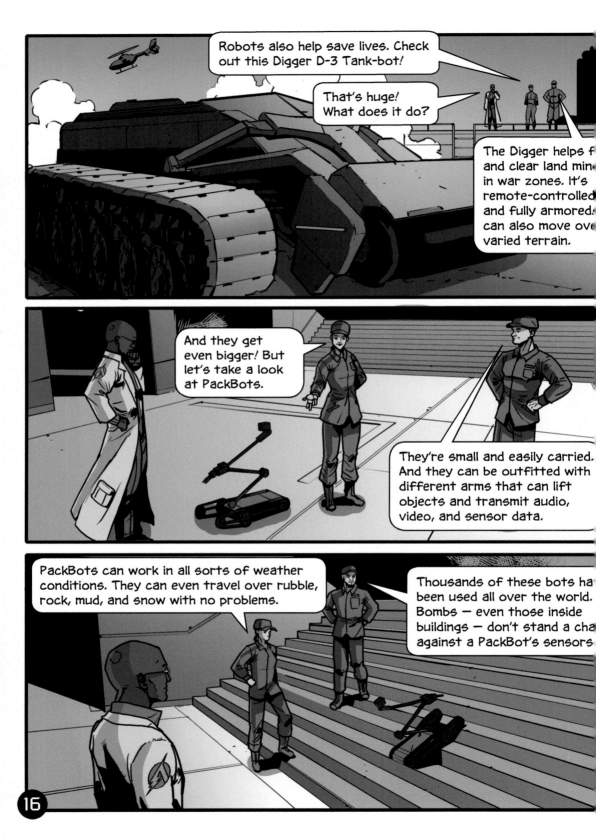

Robots also help save lives. Check out this Digger D-3 Tank-bot!

That's huge! What does it do?

The Digger helps f and clear land min in war zones. It's remote-controlled and fully armored can also move ove varied terrain.

And they get even bigger! But let's take a look at PackBots.

They're small and easily carried. And they can be outfitted with different arms that can lift objects and transmit audio, video, and sensor data.

PackBots can work in all sorts of weather conditions. They can even travel over rubble, rock, mud, and snow with no problems.

Thousands of these bots ha been used all over the world. Bombs — even those inside buildings — don't stand a cha against a PackBot's sensors

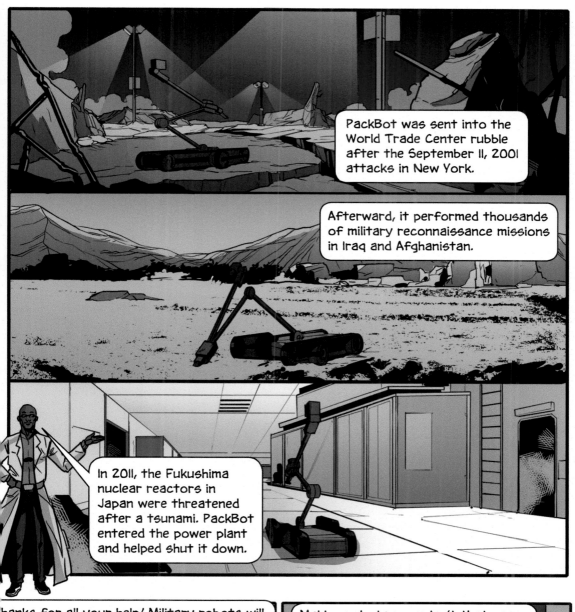

PackBot was sent into the World Trade Center rubble after the September 11, 2001 attacks in New York.

Afterward, it performed thousands of military reconnaissance missions in Iraq and Afghanistan.

In 2011, the Fukushima nuclear reactors in Japan were threatened after a tsunami. PackBot entered the power plant and helped shut it down.

hanks for all your help! Military robots will e another important part of the exhibit.

Making robots move isn't that easy. I know a lab that specializes in robot movement. I'm going to check it out!

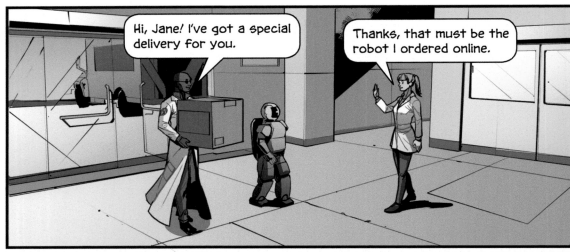

Hi, Jane! I've got a special delivery for you.

Thanks, that must be the robot I ordered online.

This is the type of robot you probably picture when you think of moving robots.

Like in sci-fi movies, right?

Right! But bipedal robots are still pretty rare. There's a lot that goes into staying upright — think how long it takes a baby to learn to walk.

FINDING THE RIGHT BALANCE

Robot designers have to figure out the right combination of movements involved in walking to program a robot's computer. Many robots have built-in balance systems that tell the computer when to correct its movements so it won't fall.

This robot looks like an insect.

Sometimes six legs can work better than two.

Six-legged robots modeled after insects have good balance and adapt well to different terrain.

Wildlife officers are using robotic taxidermied animals as bait to catch poachers. The robo-animal is placed in an area where illegal hunting might be happening. The officers hide nearby and use a remote control to operate the robot. When a poacher takes the bait, the officers act.

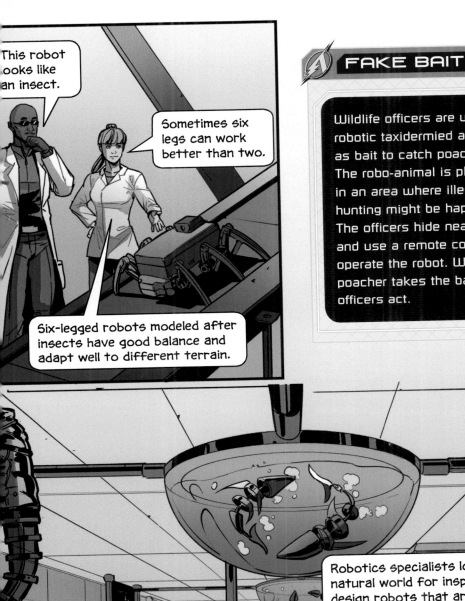

Robotics specialists look to the natural world for inspiration. They design robots that are based on animals and their movements.

Deployable Air-Land Exploration Robot (DALER)

The DALER is inspired by the vampire bat. Designed for search and rescue, it surveys the ground from above and then crawls into hard-to-reach or dangerous areas.

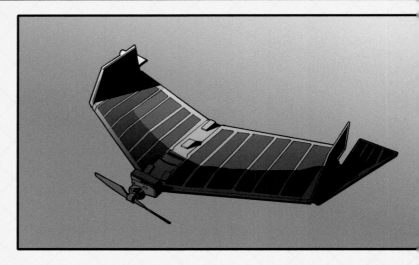

The Nano Air Vehicle

This hummingbirdlike robot can hover in the air. The fully controllable surveillance robot is used to patrol battlefields and sends video data back to its operator.

The Ghost Swimmer

The U.S. Navy's underwater drone is the size of an albacore tuna and swims like a shark. It is designed for intelligence, reconaissance, and surveillance missions.

These animal-based robots are awesome!

The Stickybot

This gecko-inspired robot was developed at Stanford University. It can walk on any smooth surface using special adhesives on its feet.

The Cheetah

The cheetah-inspired robot at Boston Dynamics is fast! It can run at speeds approaching [..] miles per hour – the fastest record land-speed times for [a] robot. The Massachusetts Institute of Technology (MIT) also has a cheetah. Moving [..]5 miles per hour, it can estimate the height, size, and distance of objects in its path, and jump over them.

The Octobot

Harvard's Octobot is the world's first entirely soft robot. Made from squishy gel, it has no power cord and uses no electronics or batteries to move. Instead, it uses gas released from chemical reactions within its "veins" to power its body.

> But what about humanoid robots? I know just the person to talk to about those.

Welcome to the social robot laboratory!

Hi, Max! How do you like my new robot?

It's unbelievable!

My job is to make robots that both look like and interact with human beings. Let's go to my lab and I can tell you all about social robots.

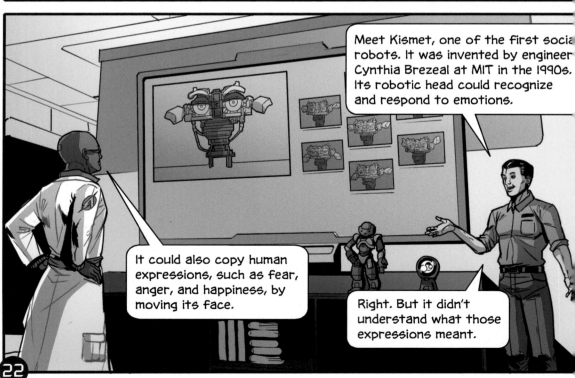

Meet Kismet, one of the first social robots. It was invented by engineer Cynthia Brezeal at MIT in the 1990s. Its robotic head could recognize and respond to emotions.

It could also copy human expressions, such as fear, anger, and happiness, by moving its face.

Right. But it didn't understand what those expressions meant.

...is robot is called Jibo. It is meant
...be a friendly assistant to families.
...xa or Siri can answer your questions,
...t Jibo can react to them and have a
...nversation with you.

Humanoid robots are built to resemble people. NAO robots can walk, talk, listen, and even recognize your face. One version of this robot is being used to help teach kids in school.

But there are robots today that look a lot more human than Kismet or Jibo.

Androids are humanoid robots with skin, hair, and realistic eyes. This one is used to welcome customers to a store in Japan. She can give directions and make conversation using a preprogrammed script.

Wow. She looks almost real.

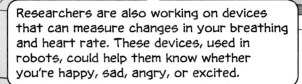

Researchers are also working on devices that can measure changes in your breathing and heart rate. These devices, used in robots, could help them know whether you're happy, sad, angry, or excited.

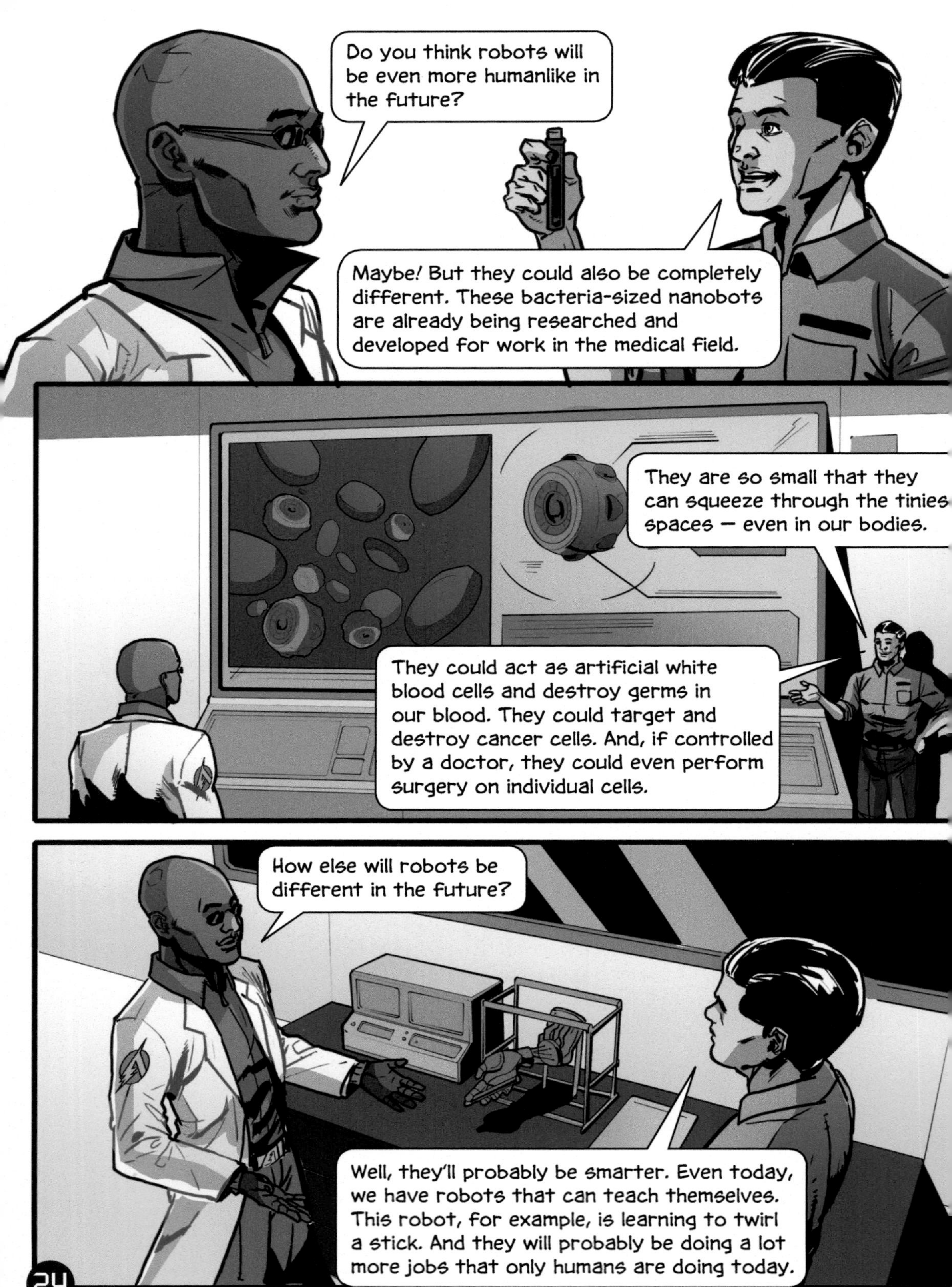
Do you think robots will be even more humanlike in the future?
Maybe! But they could also be completely different. These bacteria-sized nanobots are already being researched and developed for work in the medical field.
They are so small that they can squeeze through the tinies spaces — even in our bodies.
They could act as artificial white blood cells and destroy germs in our blood. They could target and destroy cancer cells. And, if controlled by a doctor, they could even perform surgery on individual cells.
How else will robots be different in the future?
Well, they'll probably be smarter. Even today, we have robots that can teach themselves. This robot, for example, is learning to twirl a stick. And they will probably be doing a lot more jobs that only humans are doing today.

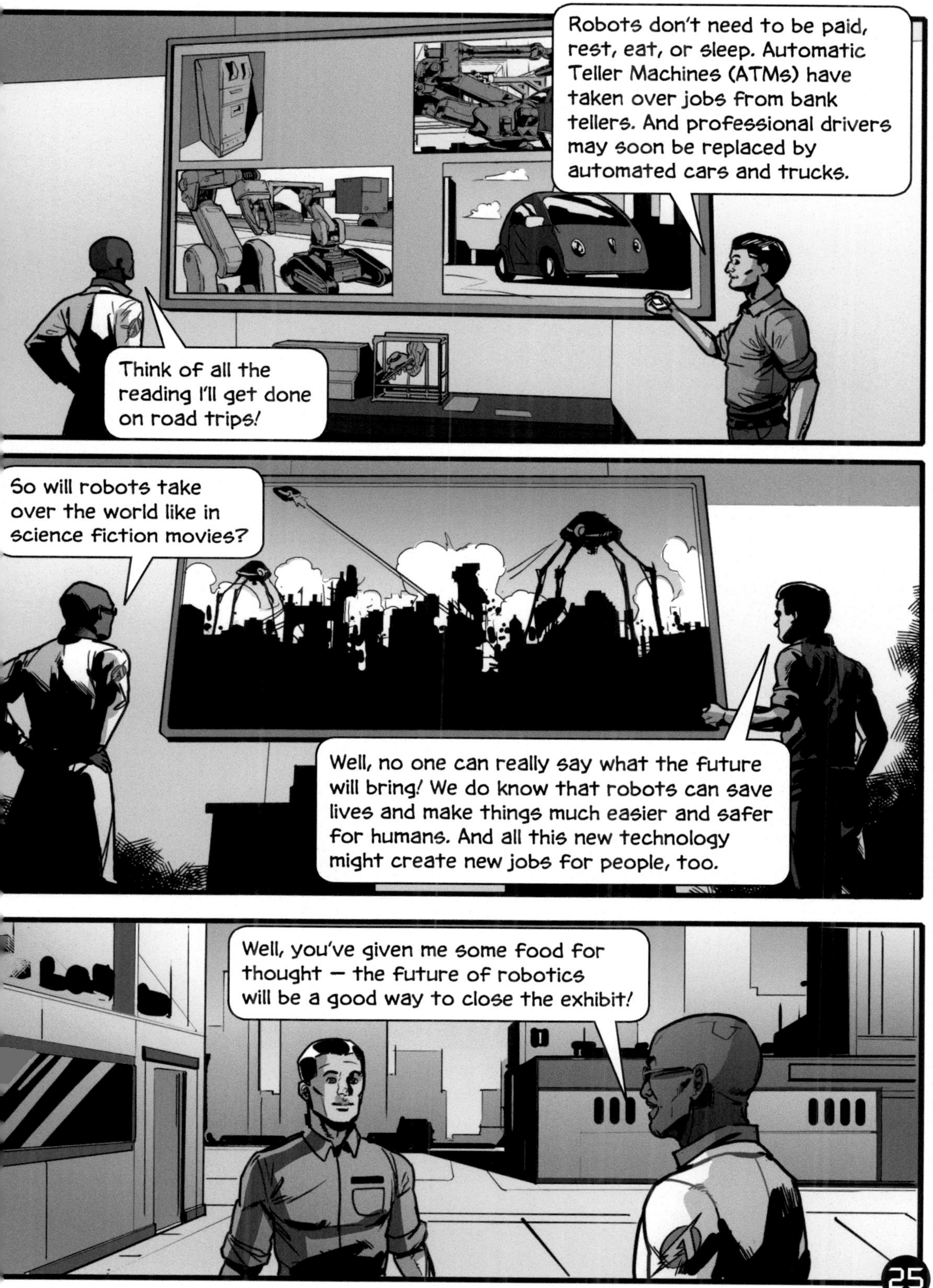
Robots don't need to be paid, rest, eat, or sleep. Automatic Teller Machines (ATMs) have taken over jobs from bank tellers. And professional drivers may soon be replaced by automated cars and trucks.
Think of all the reading I'll get done on road trips!
So will robots take over the world like in science fiction movies?
Well, no one can really say what the future will bring! We do know that robots can save lives and make things much easier and safer for humans. And all this new technology might create new jobs for people, too.
Well, you've given me some food for thought — the future of robotics will be a good way to close the exhibit!

Thanks, Max! Everything you have here is great!

We'll have displays where visitors can interact with the robots and see what they can do in person. Max, I think the exhibit is going to be a huge success — and we couldn't have done it without you.

Glad to help. And now I'm going home — it's been a long day! At least my robot cleaned the floors.

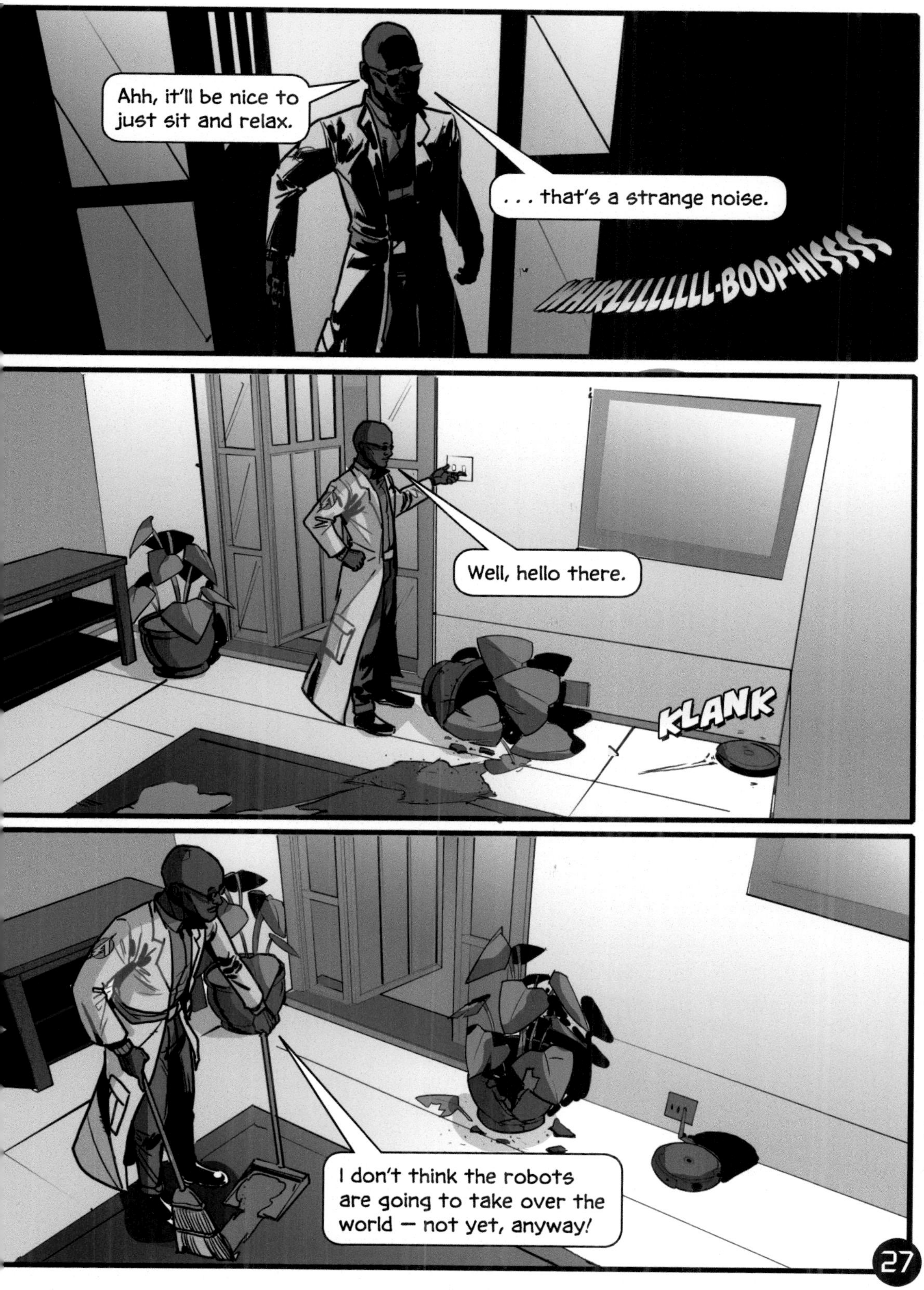

Ahh, it'll be nice to just sit and relax.
. . . that's a strange noise.
WHIRLLLLLLLLL-BOOP-HISSSS
Well, hello there.
KLANK
I don't think the robots are going to take over the world — not yet, anyway!

MORE ABOUT
ROBOTS

Some robots have sensors that allow them to smell and taste. They have been use to judge contests and even verify the authenticity of Thai food. Robots that can smell, known as "electronic noses," can be programmed to recognize the smell of alcohol, blood, urine, and sweat. These robots could be used in search-and-rescue missions, as well as to sense and warn of dangerous gas leaks.

Tiny flying robots are being developed to help pollinate crops in the future. Harvard University's RoboBee has a wingspan of 1.2 inches (3 centimeters). It can both fly and swim.

Robot cops are already patrolling our streets. Police in Cleveland, Ohio enlist the help of a robot called Griffin, a small, six-wheeled rover that can look for explosives. In Los Angeles, a robot called BatCat can pick up car bombs with a 50-foot (15.2-meter)-long arm. It can also rip through houses to end standoffs.

Lifelike robotic pets are bringing companionship and comfort to people who might not be able to care for real ones. Robotic cats that purr when stroked and robotic dogs that bark and cock their heads when spoken to are already on the market. Paro, a baby harp seal robot developed in Japan, has been used as a soothing tool in hospitals and nursing homes since 2003. Similar to a live animal, Paro is said to help reduce a patient's stress and helps patients and caregivers talk to each other.

CRITICAL THINKING QUESTIONS

1. Advanced robots that can think and act like humans are a popular subject in sci-fi books and movies. Can you think of an example of this? What happened in the story?

2. Robots are becoming more and more a part of everyday life. Does a robot help make your life easier? How so? If not, how would you incorporate a robot into your daily routine?

3. Think about robots in sci-fi films. Then compare them to the robots and artificial-intelligence programs we use today, such as Roomba, Siri, or Alexa; robots used as toys or in competitions; and military robots. How are they alike? How are they different?

MORE ABOUT

SUPER SCIENTIST

Real name: Maxwell J. Axiom
Hometown: Seattle, Washington
Height: 6' 1"   Weight: 192 lbs
Eyes: Brown   Hair: None

Super capabilities: Super intelligence; able to shrink to the size of an atom; sunglasses give x-ray vision; lab coat allows for travel through time and space.

Origin: Since birth, Max Axiom seemed destined for greatness. His mother, a marine biologist, taught her son about the mysteries of the sea. His father, a nuclear physicist and volunteer park ranger, schooled Max on the wonders of earth and sky.

One day on a wilderness hike, a megacharged lightning bolt struck Max with blinding fury. When he awoke, Max discovered a newfound energy and set out to learn as much about science as possible. He traveled the globe earning degrees in every aspect of the field. Upon his return, he was ready to share his knowledge and new identity with the world. He had become Max Axiom, Super Scientist.

GLOSSARY

android (AN-droid)—a robot that looks, thinks, and acts very similar to a human being

automate (aw-TAH-mayt)—a mechanical process that is programmed to follow a set of instructions

bipedal (BI-pe-duhl)—something that walks on two feet

hydraulic (hye-DRAW-lik)—having to do with a system powered by fluid forced through pipes or chambers

piston (PIS-tuhn)—a part inside a hydraulic machine that moves up and down to expand and compress fluid

pivot (PIV-uht)—to turn or balance on a point

pneumatic (noo-MAT-ik)—operated by compressed air

reconnaisance (ree-KAH-nuh-suhnss)—a mission to gather information about an enemy

sensor (SEN-sur)—an instrument that detects physical changes in the environment

surveillance (suhr-VAY-luhnss)—the act of keeping very close watch on someone, someplace, or something

taxidermy (TAK-suh-dur-mee)—preparing, stuffing, and mounting skins of animals to make them look alive

terrain (tuh-RAYN)—the surface of the land

tsunami (tsoo-NAH-mee)—a large, destructive wave caused by an underwater earthquake

READ MORE

Burrows, Terry. *Robots, Drones, and Radar: Electronics Go to War.* STEM on the Battlefield. Minneapolis: Lerner Publications, 2018.

Noll, Elizabeth. *Space Robots.* World of Robots. Minneapolis: Bellwether Media, Inc., 2018.

Otfinoski, Steven. *Making Robots: Science, Technology, Engineering.* Calling All Innovators. New York: Children's Press, an imprint of Scholastic Inc., 2017.

Smibert, Angie. *Building Better Robots.* Space Frontiers. North Mankato, Minn.: 12-Story Library, 2017.

INTERNET SITES

Use FactHound to find Internet sites related to this book.

Visit www.facthound.com

Just type in 9781515773917 and go.

Super-cool stuff! Check out projects, games and lots more at
www.capstonekids.com

Index